12/03

Folk Games

North American Folklore

Children's Folklore
Christmas and Santa Claus Folklore
Contemporary Folklore
Ethnic Folklore
Family Folklore
Firefighters' Folklore
Folk Arts and Crafts
Folk Customs
Folk Dance
Folk Fashion
Folk Festivals
Folk Games
Folk Medicine
Folk Music
Folk Proverbs and Riddles
Folk Religion
Folk Songs
Folk Speech
Folk Tales and Legends
Food Folklore
Regional Folklore

North American Folklore

Folk Games

BY JOYCE LIBAL

Mason Crest Publishers

Mason Crest Publishers Inc.
370 Reed Road
Broomall, Pennsylvania 19008
(866) MCP-BOOK (toll free)
www.masoncrest.com

First printing
1 2 3 4 5 6 7 8 9 10
Library of Congress Cataloging-in-Publication Data on file at the Library of Congress.
ISBN 1-59084-339-8
        1-59084-328-2 (series)

Design by Lori Holland.
Composition by Bytheway Publishing Services, Binghamton, New York.
Cover design by Joe Gilmore.
Printed and bound in the Hashemite Kingdom of Jordan.

Picture credits:
Comstock: pp. 25, 28, 30, 34, 38, 84, 86, 89, 92, 94, 97
Corel: pp. 48, 63, 100
PhotoDisc: pp. 6, 8, 14, 16, 22, 42, 46, 52, 54, 58, 60, 62, 64, 66, 70, 71
Cover: "Marbles Champ" by Norman Rockwell © 1939 SEPS: Licensed by Curtis
        Publishing, Indianapolis, IN. www.curtispublishing.com

Printed by permission of the Norman Rockwell Family
© the Norman Rockwell Family Entities

Contents

Folklore grows from long-ago
seeds. Just as an acorn sends
down roots even as it shoots up
leaves across the sky, folklore is
rooted deeply in the past and
yet still lives and grows today.
It spreads through our modern
world with branches as wide
and sturdy as any oak's;
it grounds us in yesterday even
as it helps us make sense of
both the present and the future.

Introduction

by Dr. Alan Jabbour

WHAT DO A TALE, a joke, a fiddle tune, a quilt, a jig, a game of jacks, a saint's day procession, a snake fence, and a Halloween costume have in common? Not much, at first glance, but all these forms of human creativity are part of a zone of our cultural life and experience that we sometimes call "folklore."

The word "folklore" means the cultural traditions that are learned and passed along by ordinary people as part of the fabric of their lives and culture. Folklore may be passed along in verbal form, like the urban legend that we hear about from friends who assure us that it really happened to a friend of their cousin. Or it may be tunes or dance steps we pick up on the block, or ways of shaping things to use or admire out of materials readily available to us, like that quilt our aunt made. Often we acquire folklore without even fully realizing where or how we learned it.

Though we might imagine that the word "folklore" refers to cultural traditions from far away or long ago, we actually use and enjoy folklore as part of our own daily lives. It is often ordinary, yet we often remember and prize it because it seems somehow very special. Folklore is culture we share with others in our communities, and we build our identities through the sharing. Our first shared identity is family identity, and family folklore such as shared meals or prayers or songs helps us develop a sense of belonging. But as we grow older we learn to belong to other groups as well. Our identities may be ethnic, religious, occupational, or regional—or all of these, since no one has only one cultural identity. But in every case, the identity is anchored and strengthened by a variety of cultural traditions in which we participate and

3

share with our neighbors. We feel the threads of connection with people we know, but the threads extend far beyond our own immediate communities. In a real sense, they connect us in one way or another to the world.

Folklore possesses features by which we distinguish ourselves from each other. A certain dance step may be African American, or a certain story urban, or a certain hymn Protestant, or a certain food preparation Cajun. Folklore can distinguish us, but at the same time it is one of the best ways we introduce ourselves to each other. We learn about new ethnic groups on the North American landscape by sampling their cuisine, and we enthusiastically adopt musical ideas from other communities. Stories, songs, and visual designs move from group to group, enriching all people in the process. Folklore thus is both a sign of identity, experienced as a special marker of our special groups, and at the same time a cultural coin that is well spent by sharing with others beyond our group boundaries.

Folklore is usually learned informally. Somebody, somewhere, taught us that jump rope rhyme we know, but we may have trouble remembering just where we got it, and it probably wasn't in a book that was assigned as homework. Our world has a domain of formal knowledge, but folklore is a domain of knowledge and culture that is learned by sharing and imitation rather than formal instruction. We can study it formally—that's what we are doing now!—but its natural arena is in the informal, person-to-person fabric of our lives.

Not all culture is folklore. Classical music, art sculpture, or great novels are forms of high art that may contain folklore but are not themselves folklore. Popular music or art may be built on folklore themes and traditions, but it addresses a much wider and more diverse audience than folk music or folk art. But even in the world of popular and mass culture, folklore keeps popping up around the margins. E-mail is not folklore—but an e-mail smile is. And college football is not folklore—but the wave we do at the stadium is.

This series of volumes explores the many faces of folklore throughout the North American continent. By illuminating the many aspects of folklore in our lives, we hope to help readers of the series to appreciate more fully the richness of the cultural fabric they either possess already or can easily encounter as they interact with their North American neighbors.

Ring-around-the-rosy is one of the earliest and simplest games that adults teach children.

ONE

Why People Play
The Meaning of Games

Playing games pulls people together.

WORRIED AND UNCERTAIN, Caitlin stepped into her new bedroom. Slowly, she began to unpack the treasured items she had saved over the 13 years of her life.

Her mother's new job had meant big changes for the family. Finances had improved greatly, and that allowed her parents to purchase a home in this exclusive neighborhood. Unfortunately, it also meant Caitlin would be studying at a new school beginning on Monday—and she couldn't rid her mind or body of the anxiety that thought caused. Would she like the new school? Would she be able to make friends there? What if the kids didn't like her? Would anyone talk to her? Would she have to walk to her classes alone? Would she be invited to join a group at someone's lunch table? If they didn't ask her, would she have the courage to ask them anyway? What if they said they'd rather she sat somewhere else?

To distract herself from her worries, Caitlin opened the window to let in the warm spring air. The sound of laughter also floated in.

Caitlin's window provided a view of the family's backyard, and she noticed that hardly any trees had been planted yet in this new subdivision. The yards were large and they all joined together to form a huge open space. Some kids from the neighborhood were gathering at one end. Several ages were represented in this group of girls and boys. One boy held a white and black ball. Teams formed quickly and an impromptu, and very informal, game of soccer began.

A moment later Caitlin's mother urged her to come downstairs for a glass of lemonade. The maze of new rooms were beginning to look less alien as Caitlin passed familiar furniture and pictures of family members who looked down at her from newly painted walls. As she passed through the kitchen she overheard parts of the conversation between her parents who were already on the deck. "When I met Mrs. Cooper yesterday," said Caitlin's mother, "she told me there's a bridge club in the neighborhood."

"No kidding, that's great," her father responded and then continued, "I'm anxious to see what kind of golfers we have in the neighborhood." Caitlin joined her parents on the deck and sipped her lemonade. She almost died of embarrassment when her father yelled "nice kick" to the freckle-faced boy who had just scored a goal. But she didn't remain a spectator for long because that goal prompted a girl on the opposing team to shout an invitation to Caitlin, "Hey, we're one short. Wanna play?"

All the trepidation, anxiety, and embarrassment vanished from Caitlin's mind and body as she raced across the yard to join the group. As she concentrated on the game, the only emotion she felt was happiness.

WHY do people play games? For many reasons. In Caitlin's case, she wants to make friends, to be part of a group, to feel comfortable in new surroundings, to have fun. She'll also be ridding her body of the stress caused by anxiety and fear, and she'll be gaining the health benefits of aerobic exercise while she plays. She'll be exercising her eyes and mind, too, as she closely watches the movement of the ball and other players, knowing she must react quickly to ever-changing situations.

People also play games to relieve boredom,

> **Game:** amusement, diversion, fun, sport, a procedure for gaining an end, a physical or mental competition conducted according to rules with the participants in direct opposition to each other
>
> From *Webster's Tenth New Collegiate Dictionary*.

to challenge themselves physically and mentally, to gain social acceptance, to relieve themselves of pent-up aggression, and to compete as well as to cooperate with others. Leadership skills are tested and developed when people play games. Individuals'

A game is a place where people can meet each other and demonstrate who they are without the need to ask questions or explain everything about themselves verbally. Conversation can be enjoyable, but sometimes people feel shy and awkward in new situations. A game has the power to make those feelings disappear and provides an avenue where individuals can take the first steps toward friendship.

Each person engaged in the game will learn about the strengths and weaknesses of other players. For example, generosity might be demonstrated by passing a ball to a player who is closer to a goal rather than trying to move the ball across the playing field to make a goal yourself. If someone on a team falls down, a player from an opposing team demonstrates kindness when he or she extends a hand to help that player up. To play a game is to become part of the social structure of a group, at least while the game is in progress and possibly for long after it ends. When you play a game, you share common goals with team members, you touch each other's lives, and you begin to form memories together. All of these things are important, even if they only seem to last for the duration of the game.

PLAY VS. GAMES

Children and adults engage in both play and games. Although we say we play a game, games are a little different from play. (See chapter seven for a more in-depth discussion.)

Play is spontaneous. It happens on the spur of the moment.
Games are often planned ahead of time

Play is creative. It makes up its own rules as it goes along.
Games are structured. It follows established rules that are based on tradition.

Play is different every day.
Games may change over the years, but they evolve slowly. In many cases, they stay basically the same for centuries.

Play is free flowing, with little structure.
Games are structured.

Play may be the inspiration for games, but games are the traditions that endure as part of our folklore.

confidence can grow, and as that happens, they often become more assertive.

Human beings don't only play games during childhood and adolescence. Caitlin's parents are also hoping to meet new friends who will enjoy participating in the kinds of games they like.

When did all of this playing begin? What was the first game and who played it? We don't really know. People have been playing games throughout recorded history. Games probably began very early in our development. Can you imagine what the first game might have been? Perhaps it was a rock-throwing contest, or a footrace to the river, or wrestling of some sort. All of these are possible, for they are all among the earliest of games.

Very young children play alone—but as they get older, learning to play with others is one of the important skills they acquire.

TWO

A Cross-Cultural Language

Using Games to Communicate

People who play games together share a bond that needs no common verbal language.

DAVE PULLED his hands away from his face, uncovering his eyes; he was surprised to hear the high tone of his voice as he cried, "Peekaboo!" The little face that peered up at him gurgled in surprise and delight, encouraging Dave to repeat his antics.

Several thoughts raced through Dave's mind as the game continued. This new father's love swelled as did his curiosity. Dave thought he knew himself pretty well, but playing with his first child was teaching him that, even at his age, there were new discoveries about himself to be made. Dave's friends considered him to be a pretty macho guy. "Wouldn't they be surprised to hear me now," Dave thought as he wondered why he was speaking to his baby in such a high-pitched, sort of "singsongy" voice. "Well, I don't know why I'm talking this way, but I'm having fun. And you are, too, aren't you, baby? Do you want to play peekaboo some more? Do you?" Dave covered his eyes, smiling already at the delight he knew he'd feel as the game continued. The baby couldn't answer her father or even understand the words being spoken. But she was playing the game as actively as her father—and without any conscious effort she was learning important lessons.

FOR most of us, game playing begins in infancy with hand and rhyme games and continues through adulthood. Do you remember playing peekaboo or "Itsy Bitsy Spider"? Chances are games like this were among your initiation to the world of play. When you were a little older you probably played ring-around-the-rosie and duck, duck, goose with other small children. These

Snowy climates have their own set of games, including tobogganing, a word that comes from the Algonquin language.

games provide early lessons in **socialization** for the children playing them.

Children have been playing these games for many, many years. When children participate in these activities, children learn that there is pleasure in the company of their parents and peers. They practice taking turns, which provides lessons in fairness. They learn to trust others. These simple games require nothing more than willing participants.

Some childhood games, like button, button, who's got the button, require only the simplest equipment (a button and some hiding places). Two participants and a piece of string are all that is needed for cat's cradle. Have you ever played tiddleywinks? This old game is played with several small disks and

Sometimes the tools cultures have developed to cope with climate have been used in the development of a game or sport. For instance, the word *toboggan* comes from an Algonquian word *odabaggan*. Native American hunters used toboggans to carry their catch over the snow-covered landscape, and they probably used them for play and sport, too, just as we do today.

Hockey is another example of a climate-related sport. Can you think of others?

one large disk. With the large disk, players press down on an edge of a small disk in order to pop the small disk into a cup or small container. The first person to get all of their disks in the cup wins. Even simple games like these can provide hours of enjoyment.

Almost any object can be used to create a game, and the participants can make up the rules of a game as they go along. For example, do you remember this humorous passage from the **classic** tale of *Tom Sawyer*?

Tom appeared on the side-walk with a bucket of white-wash and a long-handled brush. He surveyed the fence, and the gladness went out of nature, and a deep melancholy settled down upon his spirit. Thirty yards of broad fence nine feet high! It seemed to him that life was hollow, and existence a burden. . . . Tom surveyed his last touch with the eye of an artist; then he gave his brush another gentle sweep, and surveyed the results as before. Ben ranged up alongside of him. Tom's mouth watered for the apple, but he stuck to his work. Ben said:

"Hello old chap; you got to work, hey?"

"Why, it's you, Ben! I warn't noticing."

"Say, I'm going in a swimming, I am. Don't you wish you could? But of course, you'd druther work, wouldn't you? 'Course you would!"

Tom contemplated the boy a bit, and said, "What do you call work?"

"Why, ain't that work?"

Tom resumed his whitewashing, and answered carelessly:

"Well, maybe it is, and maybe it ain't. All I know is, it suits Tom Sawyer."

"Oh, come now, you don't mean to let on that you like it?"

The brush continued to move.

"Like it? Well, I don't see why I oughtn't to like it. Does a boy get a chance to whitewash a fence every day?"

That put the thing in a new light. Ben stopped nibbling his apple. Tom swept his brush daintily back and forth—stepped back to note the effect—added a touch here and there—criticized the effect again, Ben watching every move, and getting more and more interested, more and more absorbed. Presently he said:

"Say, Tom, let me whitewash a little.". . . Tom gave up the brush with reluctance in his face, but alacrity in his heart. . . . Boys happened along every little while; they came to jeer, but remained to whitewash. . . . Tom said to himself that it was not such a hollow world after all. He had discovered a great law of human action, without knowing it, namely, that, in order to make a man or a boy covet a thing, it is only necessary to make the thing difficult to attain. If he had been a great and wise philosopher, like the writer of this book, he would now have comprehended that work consists of whatever a body is obliged to do, and that play consists of whatever a body is not obliged to do. . . .

This peek into the life of Tom Sawyer illustrates the point that any activity can indeed be turned into a game—even a tiresome chore.

Many games rely on the simplest materials and activities. Remember the jump rope games you played as a child? Many adults still jump rope for the exercise it provides—and all you

Test your game-making ingenuity:

Conduct a game-designing contest. Have each of your friends work independently to develop a game. To make it really fun, require that at least one household object be utilized in the game. Ask each person to explain the rules of his/her game, and then take turns playing each of them.

really need is the right length of rope. Have you ever played pick-up sticks? This simple game requires only a pile of sticks to drop on the ground. Players take turns, and the point of the game is to pick up as many sticks as possible. But each time you pick up a stick, you must do it without moving any of the others. If you move one of the other sticks, you lose your turn.

Unlike jump rope or pick-up sticks, which are classic historical games, many games are made up by children on the spur of the moment, using materials at hand. Some games endure and become part of our folk tradition, but others are temporary games. They may only be played once or never be played by more than a single group of participants.

The majority of well-known games we play as children, however, have been played for centuries. Nevertheless, there must have been a time when each of these games did not exist, and there must have been one individual or group who created that game. We do not know the exact origins of many common games. They are simply a part of our folk heritage, passed along from generation to generation.

Some games played by children in the United States and Canada are derived from those played by children in other countries. The reason for this is that the United States and Canada were settled by **immigrants**, and these people brought games and other traditions with them when they arrived on the New World's shores. But even countries that do not have large immigrant populations often have games similar to those played in other countries. Folk traditions—including games—seem to somehow travel through the air by invisible and inexplicable means. Sometimes historians can tell where a game originated; other times it's difficult to determine the place of origin.

Perhaps you remember playing some of the following games or games that are very similar to them. Some type of object is

needed to play each of these games—and each game originated
in a different part of the world.

SOUTH AFRICA

The ancient game of hopscotch is thousands of years old, and
variations of it are played in many countries. Marcia Ball of Um-
tali, Zimbabwe, explained a South African version of the game to

*Hopscotch is thousands of years old and played
around the world.*

Children in North America have jumped rope since colonial days. The game is also played in other countries.

Canadian Nina Millen for inclusion in her book *Children's Games from Many Lands*. The South African children call the game tsetsetse and play it by drawing a rectangular grid in the sand. This version of the game involves placing a stone in one of the rectangles, hopping on one foot, and kicking the stone into successive rectangles with the same foot.

BRAZIL

In this South American country, children play a game called *gato mia* (cat meow). One child, who is blindfolded, has to find other children in a room. When the blindfolded child touches someone, he says, "Cat, meow." The touched child must meow, and the blindfolded child tries to guess who is the meowing child.

UKRAINE

Here's a skipping rope game from Ukraine that's the same as a North American jump rope game. A rope is stretched between two people who turn it. Other participants stand in a line and must skip through the rope in sequence. Each time a person has a turn, she or he must jump over the rope in a more difficult way. The first time one jumps with both feet, the second time on one leg, and it gets progressively harder. Perhaps the next time the child will have to enter backward, for example. When a participant gets caught in the rope, she must start over with the easiest jumping level.

Ukrainian children also play a ball game similar to one you may have played at parties or in school. For this game, a group stands in a circle. One person holds a small ball (a tennis ball works well for this) between his chin and his chest. The object of the game is to pass the ball from one person to another without touching it with your hands. When the ball is dropped, the person who drops it must leave the game. The last person remaining wins.

NORTH AMERICA

Marbles have been a prized possession for generations, and playing with them was among the most popular activities for children in colonial times. Our ancestors also liked a game called ringtaw, and you can play it too. Use a stick to draw two circles on the ground, one inside of the other. Put several small marbles inside the smallest circle. Then "shoot" a large marble from outside of the largest circle toward a small marble. The goal is to knock the small marbles out of the circle, and the person who knocks the most marbles out of the circle wins.

Most games played in colonial times required little, if any, equipment. For example, one old game required only one small hoop and a stick for each participant. Each person (usually a girl)

Marbles were prized possessions and a fascinating game for colonial children.

This child's set of card dates from the 1700s.

would use her stick to toss the hoop to another participant who had to catch the hoop with her stick.

TODAY, these games from other places and other times continue to be enjoyed by children across North America. Game traditions link us to one another, spanning the barriers of geography and time.

Next time you have to spend a few hours with someone who seems very different from you, try playing a game together. You may find you don't need to share common interests or even a common language. Games create connections between people, connections that are independent of culture. We don't need to say a word to play a game together. Even the simplest game forms a common "language" we all can understand.

Dominoes is a "parlor game" whose name comes from a Latin phrase meaning "let us bless the Lord."

THREE

In the Parlor
Games for Rainy Afternoons

The parlor game of checkers has been played in North American since the 18th century.

JASON AWOKE to the sound of rain pelting the window-panes in his bedroom and felt gloom descend upon him like a ton of bricks. "Why oh why does it have to rain on Saturday?" he muttered as he tried to will himself back to sleep.

His mother's voice calling him to breakfast put an end to any thoughts of sleeping this awful, depressing day away. Jason walked to the kitchen with heavy steps. Even the tantalizing aroma of blueberry pancakes (one of his favorite foods) didn't lighten his mood. "This day was ruined before it began," he said under his breath as he sat down at the table.

Jason's father began singing that *Don't Worry, Be Happy* song, inserting Jason's name into the lyrics, but the song just made Jason even more ill-tempered. "I can't believe you're singing," Jason said. "Have you looked outside?"

"Come on, Jason," his father implored, "It's Saturday! What's a little rain?"

"That's right." Jason agreed. Then he continued, "It's Saturday. The most important day of the week. It's not going to be Saturday again for seven whole days! Baseball is going to be cancelled now! I'm not going to get to see my friends! There's nothing to do now. This day is about as exciting as a pile of dog poop."

"Jason." His mother's mouth pinched with disapproval. "Watch your mouth, young man."

"Sorry. But I'm upset. What am I going to do now?"

"You could help me clean the basement," his father suggested.

"Oh great! I can't play baseball, but I can help clean the basement. That's just great. Now I feel fantastic."

"Sarcasm won't get you very far in life, Jason," his mother said. Then she turned to answer the phone. "Jason, it's for you."

Jason's heart was heavy as he said, "Hello. . . Oh, Pete. . . What's up? . . . Yeah, I know baseball's cancelled. I've been looking out the window. . . Sure.

"Mom, can Pete come over this afternoon?"

"Sure. She said it's fine. . . Okay, I'll see you at one."

When Pete arrived, Jason had already helped his father clean the basement and was now seated in front of the television playing a video game. "Wrestling, great, let me choose a guy," Pete said as he grabbed a set of controls and selected from among the available wrestlers. Pete and Jason were totally engrossed in the game when lightning cracked and the accompanying thunder rumbled so loudly the house shook. "OH NO!" the boys cried in unison as the electricity went out.

"I can't believe it!" Jason threw down the controls.

"It's not going to make the day better if you break the video controls, Jason," his father said.

"Well, what are we going to do now? There's nothing to do here without electricity," Jason complained.

Jason's father stepped into his bedroom for a moment and returned with a deck of cards. "I think you boys will enjoy this. Margie, why don't you join us?" he said as they walked into the kitchen and sat down at the table. Jason's mother brought cookies and milk to the table.

Although the boys were skeptical at first, by the time the day ended they had to admit they'd had a great afternoon. Go fish, slapjack, even snip-snap-snorem—there seemed to be no end to the goofy card games Jason's mom and dad knew. They didn't even stop playing when the rain ended and the electricity came back on a few hours later. Instead, Jason's dad ordered a pizza to be delivered so his mom wouldn't have to stop playing cards to make dinner.

When the day was over, Pete and Jason said their good-byes at the front door. "You know, I never realized how cool your parents are, Jason. I had a great time today," Pete exclaimed.

"Yeah, me too," Jason agreed. "I thought Mom was practically going to jump on top of the table when she won at go fish." The boys laughed. "See you Monday," they said in unison, and they laughed again.

Before going to bed that evening, Jason stuck his head in the living room where his mom and dad were watching television. "Thanks," he said. "Pete and I had a great time today."

"We enjoyed it too," Jason's dad said, and his mom nodded her head in agreement as she kissed Jason good night.

HAVE you ever had an experience similar to Jason's? In days past, spending rainy days playing games around a table was a more common practice than it is today. The living room was called the parlor, and games people played indoors were often referred to as parlor games. These games were played as a social pastime when company was visiting, when it was too dark to continue working outside, and when inclement weather made playing outdoors impossible.

Playing cards is one of the all-time favorite parlor games. Everyone agrees that people have been playing card games for thousands of years, but no one knows exactly when the first cards were developed. Some historians think it may have been soon after people learned how to draw! Other historians think cards were invented by the Chinese, or the Egyptians, or people living in Babylonia. We do know that playing cards were popular in Italy by the 1300s.

Cards can be used for a variety of games, from poker to go fish.

Playing cards from the 16th century.

But cards did not always look the way our standard deck looks today. Over the centuries the **suits** (what today we call clubs, hearts, spades, and diamonds) have been represented by many different objects, including elephants, birds, leaves, and flowers. Still today, some countries have decks with cards numbering less than 52 (our standard).

In the 1800s, however, many parents in America didn't allow their children to play with decks that had numbers and suits. Some conservative religious groups today still forbid "face cards." That's because they think this type of deck might encourage

Instead of the customary suits we use today, these playing cards from the middle of the 17th century used flowers, fruits, and animals.

In times past, playing cards were often different shapes than they are today.

Playing cards from the 1860s.

gambling. Instead, children often play with bright, colorful decks made specifically for card games like old maid.

This simple game, created in the 1800s, is all about matching pairs. It can be played with any standard deck as long as you remove one of the queens so that the one that matches it can be used to represent

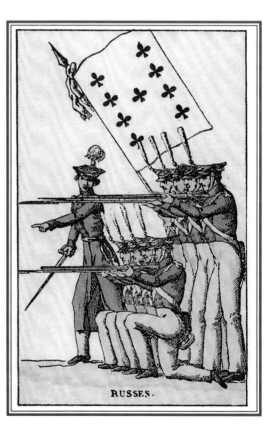

In the 1600s, these playing cards were used for a parlor game called "game of the flags."

the old maid. If you remove a king, you can play old bachelor. But it's even more fun, and easier for very young children, if you have a specialty deck of cards. With these decks you match pictures instead of numbers. Specialty decks were popular in America long ago, and they are still being produced today.

Along with card games like old maid, back in the 1800s there were also educational decks of cards that were used to teach various school subjects such as geography and history. Decks filled with interesting characters have been

DICE

The common dice we use today have six sides, but dice were designed in various styles in different countries and cultures. Games played with two-sided dice were popular among some groups of Native Americans. Four-sided dice and pyramid-shaped dice were also used for games by different people.

Dice have been used for centuries—both for determining how many spaces to move on a board game and for gambling.

around a very long time, and some of them are now prized by antique collectors.

Educational board games were also popular, but often children did not use dice to determine how many spaces to move forward. That's because some parents thought dice could also encourage gambling. Instead, children would spin an arrow on a dial. The number of spaces to move on the board would be determined by the number on which the arrow landed. Or the child would spin a "teetotum" to determine the number of spaces to move.

A teetotum was a sort of top with flat sides. Each side displayed a number or dots (like dice). When the teetotum fell on its side, the number facing up would be the number of spaces to move.

Backgammon was a popular parlor game as were checkers and chess; all have been favored board games throughout American history. People in ancient Greece and Egypt played checker games that were similar to the game we play today. Some histori-

FANT

You might enjoy playing this Ukrainian game with a group of friends. Blindfold one person and select someone to act as assistant. The assistant holds a hat or a bag into which each player places one small personal item (a watch, ring, hair clip, earring, etc.). The blindfolded person reaches into the hat or bag, removes one item not knowing who it belongs to, and says, "This *Fant* has to [here she or he names whatever it is that the owner of the item has to do. The person might have to sing a song, or crawl while howling, etc].

ans think that chess originated in India, but others say chess was first played in the area that is now Iran as early as the sixth century AD. These historians think the game spread from the Middle East to India and later to China. In the tenth century it arrived in Europe, and the Europeans were the ones who brought chess to America.

People have devised many different ways to play chess, but the rules that are most common can be easily learned. Chess is a more intellectual game than checkers, however. People in many countries study chess and play it in tournaments, making it truly an international game.

DESIGN A BOARD GAME

Gather the following supplies: a large piece of poster board, a ruler or yardstick, a pencil, and paints or colored markers. Use the pencil and ruler or yardstick to section off into squares the various components of your game on the poster board. Then paint or use the markers to write words, draw objects, and color in the sections as desired. You'll need dice or some other means of determining how many spaces a player can move on any given turn. If you don't have dice, the method you use might be as simple as writing numbers on small pieces of paper and putting them in an envelope. Each player could reach in and pull out a paper indicating the number of spaces to move. (This is just one suggestion. You'll probably come up with lots more.) You'll also need some type of tokens so each player will be able to mark her or his spot on the board.

Playing cards have changed over the years. The card on the left is from the late 1700s, while the card on the right, which looks like our cards today, was manufactured at the end of the 19th century.

After all, as we pointed out in the last chapter, you don't need to speak the same language to play a game together; you only need to know the rules of the game. And everyone needs something to occupy those rainy Saturdays that come along!

NATIVE AMERICAN "PARLORS"

In days past, to alleviate boredom during long winter evenings, some groups of Native Americans played a "parlor" game that involved hiding a bone within their tepee. One team tried to distract the other team by singing songs and making hand movements in order to keep the other side from finding the bone. Another game involved hiding a stick or bone in one hand, while the opposite team guessed which hand held the hidden object. This "hand game" was a gambling game with a musical accompaniment.

Because of our friendship with animals, we have included them in some of our games.

FOUR

Our Four-Footed
Friends Join the Party
Animals' Role in Games

Cowboys sometimes broke up the monotony of their workdays by riding the animals they herded. This informal game eventually turned into today's rodeo.

BACK IN THE 19th century, Lewis Carroll created a famous scene where animals were *literally* a part of the game:

> . . . *Alice thought she had never seen such a curious croquet ground in her life; it was all ridges and furrows; the croquet balls were live hedgehogs, and the mallets live flamingoes, and the soldiers had to double themselves up and stand on their hands and feet, to make the arches.*
>
> *The chief difficulty Alice found at first was in managing her flamingo; she succeeded in getting its body tucked away, comfortably enough, under her arm, with its legs hanging down; but generally, just as she had got its neck nicely straightened out, and was going to give the hedgehog a blow with its head, it would twist itself round and look up into her face with such a puzzled expression that she could not help bursting out laughing; and when she had got its head down and was going to begin again, it was very provoking to find that the hedgehog had unrolled itself, and was in the act of crawling away; besides all this, there was generally a ridge or a furrow in the way wherever she wanted to send the hedgehog to, and, as the doubled-up soldiers were always getting up and walking off to other parts of the ground, Alice came to the conclusion that it was a very difficult game indeed.*

In this whimsical game, animals play unusual and important roles. If you've ever seen old Flintstone cartoons, this passage from *Alice* may make you think of the silly prehistoric animals who function in place of all sorts of household objects. In real life, of course, we don't involve animals in our games quite so literally. But animals definitely do have roles to play in the traditional games of our folk heritage.

Take a look, for instance, at this passage from an early McGuffey's Reader:

McGuffey Readers were the books used to teach children how to read, write, and spell during the 19th century.

If they have no real animals to play with, children sometimes include imaginary animals in their games.

. . . James and Robert have gone into the shade of a high wall to play ball.

Mary and Lucy have come up from the pond near by, with brave old Ponto, to see them play.

When they toss the ball up in the air, and try to catch it, Ponto runs to get it in his mouth.

Now the ball is lost. They all look for it under the trees and in the grass; but they can not see it. Where can it be?

See! Ponto has found it. Here he comes with it. He will lay it at little Lucy's feet, or put it in her hand.

If you've ever played "fetch" with your dog, then you've shared the game experience described here.

Humans are social beings. While there are times when we want to be alone, more often we like to interact with others. Usually the "others" we interact with are also people, but this is not always the case.

Some children live in rural areas not populated by neighborhoods filled with children of a similar age. A child living in an area like this may have a pet that often takes an active role in the games the child plays. Even in a city filled with children, a favored pet may be a player in childhood games. Animals have

been the companions of human beings for centuries, and relationships people have with them are very important. We develop responsibility when we play with and care for an animal and learn to be sensitive to its needs.

Horses and humans have worked—and played—together for centuries.

Perhaps you have pulled a string away from a kitten and had a good time watching the kitten chase you and the string. Maybe you own a bird you have taught to come when you call it by name so it can be allowed to occasionally fly free in your home. Or maybe you play Frisbee with your dog. Dogs playing Frisbee with their owners have become a familiar sight in some American parks.

Dogs are among the many animals that have been used for centuries to carry heavy loads for people. In northern Canada and Alaska, dogs are still used to pull sleds filled with supplies across the snow. It is not surprising that people living in these cold climates would move this activity from purely work to pleasure by developing dogsled races. The Iditarod, held annually in Alaska, is the most well-known dog race with the dogs traveling hundreds of miles over ice and snow.

Human beings enjoy their association with animals, and from earliest times we've been involving them in selected games. The Greeks introduced horseback racing into their annual Olympian games in 648 BC. That sounds early, but the racing of chariots pulled by four horses had already been part of the games more than 300 years before that! Horseback racing has been popular in America since the beginning of colonization, and it's still a favorite pastime for many people. The annual Kentucky Derby is a highly anticipated national event.

Racing isn't the only game people have played involving

horses. In Europe during the middle ages, a ruler would some-times call for a tournament to be held. With blunted swords or lances in hand, participants would ride their steeds toward each other and try to knock the opponent off his horse. The popularity of this sport has ebbed and flowed over the centuries. This event was not conducted in the United States in colonial times, but today you might say it is gaining in popularity as manifested by the many Renaissance fairs that have cropped up across the country. There, attendees can indulge their imaginations fully in the costumes, food, and pageantry of the Middle Ages. They can observe modern-day **jousting** and even participate in some of these games.

The human mind seems to seek ways to play with everything it encounters. Just as today we find ways to play with our newest work tool—the computer and other electronic devices—in times past, we created ways to play with the animals who helped us work. Today, those games are still active parts of our game traditions.

The playground has always provided fertile soil for the growth of children's games.

FIVE

You're "It!"—and Other Childhood Pastimes
Our Heritage of Children's Games

A sack race is a game from the 1800s. It's still fun today!

WHY DO I have to be 'It?'" Rebecca complained to her older sister Angela and their friend Kim who had just spent the night at their home.

"Because somebody has to be 'It,'" Angela calmly insisted.

"Well, why me? It's always me. Every time we play, I have to be 'It.' It's not fair." Rebecca stuck out her lower lip.

"Okay, okay. I'll be 'It,'" Angela gave in as she took her place between Rebecca and Kim, who were standing at opposite ends of the bedroom. Angela raised her arms into the air and began to bob and weave from side to side as Rebecca and Kim tossed a piece of clothing to each other while trying to keep it away from Angela.

"Girls, that's enough now. The cow is waiting to be milked," called their mother.

The girls put on their sweaters quickly. While passing through the kitchen, they picked up the clean bucket, and hurried out to the barn where Lily the cow was waiting impatiently for milking to begin. When the bucket was full, Angela said, "How about one quick game of hide-and-seek before we go back to the house? Rebecca, you're 'It.'"

Rebecca sighed heavily, "Okay, but you can only hide in the barn. Everything else is off limits." Angela and Kim agreed, so Rebecca buried her face in her arm as she leaned against the barn wall and began to count quickly, "1, 2, 3 . . . 11, 12, 13 . . . 19, 20. Ready or not, here I come."

Because the barn was small, Rebecca found Angela and Kim after only a few minutes. The girls returned to the house for a quick breakfast. Mother had already packed their lunches, so there was time for a leisurely walk to school.

Children were arranged according to age in the one-room schoolhouse, which meant Rebecca sat with her friend Sarah near the front of the class. The morning passed quickly because Miss Stuart conducted a surprise spelling bee. She divided the class into two groups. Each team had the same number of students with every age and ability being represented. Miss Stuart chose appropriately difficult words for each student. The groups stood across from each other on opposite sides of the room. Rebecca ended up on the losing team, but she spelled her words correctly until the very end, so she felt good about her performance.

"Red Rover at recess," Jimmy Weido whispered just as Miss Stuart announced it was time to go outside.

Rebecca dawdled in her seat, and Sarah urged her to hurry, "Come on, they're already picking teams."

"What's the rush?" Rebecca replied. "You know Jimmy and Will are going to be the captains, and we're going to be the last ones picked, like always."

Rebecca was right. While the littlest children played on their own at the opposite end of the schoolyard, Sarah and Rebecca were the youngest kids allowed to participate in Red Rover—but because they were the smallest, they were picked last. Rebecca thought it was a cruel trick of nature that every time a game required someone to be "It," she seemed to be elected; yet every time there was a captain, she wasn't old enough or respected enough to be selected; and every time a game required teams, she

GAMES THAT TEACH

In the 1900s, spelling bees were an important school game that helped children learn to spell. Today teachers still learn games—including computer games—to help make learning fun.

was picked last because she was small. But she did want to play, so she followed Sarah outside.

"We'll take Sarah, and you can have Rebecca," Jimmy was saying just as the girls exited the building. Rebecca cringed as she heard his words, but she walked over and linked hands with Susan who was at the end of the line that comprised Will's team.

The two lines of children stood facing each other with some distance between them. The children in each line held hands tightly as Jimmy called out, "Red Rover, Red Rover, send someone over. Red Rover, Red Rover, send Rebecca over."

Rebecca was expecting it, because, not wanting their line to be broken, each captain would choose the children they perceived to be the weakest for the first runs. Rebecca had, therefore, already been gathering her courage as she prepared to run across the distance separating the teams. *I'm stronger than you know*, she thought as she took her first steps. *I'm as strong as Mr. McCeaver's bull. I'm as strong as a mountain lion.* She felt herself gaining speed. *I'm the strongest kid in this school*, she thought while gathering every ounce of strength she possessed and hurling herself into the locked hands of Sarah and Tim Delaney. Rebecca's little body bounced right off Tim's hand, and she found herself lying on the ground. Of course she had selected that particular set of hands hoping Sarah would be the weakest link in the chain, but Tim had managed to hang on to Sarah. If Rebecca had succeeded in breaking through, she would have

RED ROVER, RED ROVER

Immigrants from the former Soviet Union play this same game—except they call it Pioneer. It is played exactly as it is in America except that the captain of a team says, "Leader, Leader, give us a pioneer" (English translation).

been allowed to pick either Sarah or Tim to join her team. But, since she failed, she had to join theirs. She was about to take Sarah's hand when Tim stopped her.

"No, Rebecca, take my other hand. I'm stronger. I'll be able to hang on to you and keep the others from breaking through."

Rebecca knew Tim was right. If she held Sarah's hand, the next person over would break through them for sure. Rebecca appreciated Tim's strategy, and in the end, their team won. Angela was on the losing team. Rebecca had to admit that made her

Children may learn as much about getting along with others on the playground as they do in the classroom.

"It"

Some games have each player participating in the exact same activity. Other games have one player who is "It." For the time of the game that the player is "It," that person does not perform the same activity as the other players. Here are two examples of "It" games played by immigrants from South America:

Cabra Cega (Blind Nanny Goat)

"It" wears a blindfold as she or he tries to find the other children standing around. Those children try to escape from the blind nanny goat. When someone is touched by "It," the touched person becomes the new blind nanny goat.

Turkey

A group of children stand in a circle. "It" stands in the middle. The children toss the ball to each other while trying to keep it away from the turkey. If the turkey ("It") catches the ball, she or he changes places with the child who threw it.

Can you think of similar traditional American games?

a little bit happy. She guessed it was because she lost so many games to her older sister when they played at home.

That night at dinner Rebecca enjoyed telling her mother and father about the spelling bee and the Red Rover game.

Her mother smiled. "Speaking of games, Rebecca, it's your birthday in two weeks, and I've been wondering what games you might want to play at your party."

"That's easy," Rebecca responded. "For once in my life, I don't want to play any games where there's an 'It' or that have a captain. Let's bob for apples."

"Bobbing for apples it is," her father said. "There are plenty of apples free for the picking in late September. And your mother and I will try to think of more games that don't have an 'It' or a captain. This will be your best party ever."

GAMES play an important part in any child's life. When children play, they are not simply amusing themselves. They are also learning important lessons they will use elsewhere in life. When baby animals play, they are practicing the skills they will one day use to hunt and feed themselves—and when human

Other environments—like the beach—offer opportunities for children to exercise their imaginations and create new informal games.

children play, they too are learning what they need to be successful in life. You might say that play is a child's work.

Some games help children develop physically, but many also build their mental capacity. For instance, researchers have studied American children playing tic-tac-toe. The children who won tic-tac-toe tournaments went on to become group leaders—not because of their physical strength but because they were perceived by the other children to have good ideas. They were good at problem-solving strategies.

Researchers have also discovered that cultures with a greater number of games train their children to have a wider *repertory* of responses in their future lives. The playful child also tends to be a creative child—and creative adults are good at finding solutions to their society's problems.

Games also teach children how to cooperate with others. Some games tend to be competitive in nature, but other games offer different options. For instance, there are no winners in African American ring games, but the group works together to affirm identity, as this clapping poem demonstrates:

I ain't been to Frisco.
And I ain't been to school.
I ain't been to college.
But I ain't no fool.

From the time children begin playing together, they organize themselves into games. At the preschool and early elementary age, these may be simple singing games, like "Farmer in the Dell," ring-around-the-rosy, and "In and Out the Window." As they get older, they will progress to hopscotch and hide-and-seek. By the time they are teenagers, in today's world they will be

FOUR-SQUARE RULES

Make a square and number the squares one through four. The game begins with number one dropping the ball and hitting it underhanded into any of the other squares. The person standing in that square lets the ball bounce in the square, before hitting it underhanded to any other square. The game continues until the ball is hit out of bounds or a player cannot retrieve the ball. If the player in square number one loses, each of the players move up one square and a new number one comes into play. Player number one moves to square four.

Around the world, the language of games is the language of friendship.

playing computer games, board games, and sports. But games continue to be a vital part of young people's lives.

And don't worry. Games will still be important to you when you are an adult.

The game of basketball can be enjoyed informally, by friends having a good time together; it is also a popular professional sport.

SIX

From Games to Sports
Rules, Officials, and Spectators

Running is one of the earliest and simplest of games. Today it has become a means of exercise—and a competition sport.

NATHAN LOVED exerting his body, breaking out in a sweat, pushing himself to the limit, feeling the air rush across his skin. He had felt this way for as far back as he could remember. His mother said that Nathan had never really learned to walk; instead he learned to run, and he had been running everywhere since he was a toddler.

When Nathan was in elementary school, he and the other kids in the neighborhood regularly challenged each other to races. "Race you to the flagpole. Race you to Billie's house. Race you to the store." Phrases like these were constantly uttered by Nathan and his friends, and they were always followed by an informal race between two or more of the children. Nathan often won, and he always enjoyed the fun of the activity. That's why he joined the high school track team as soon as he was eligible to do so.

From the moment he first put it on, Nathan felt excited to be wearing the team uniform, and he longed for the day when the school booster club would hand him a varsity letter. He could imagine the letter on his school jacket, and he knew he'd be proud to wear it. Everyone who saw it would understand that he was an athlete and a part of a team.

Nathan had always been known as the fastest runner in the neighborhood—but the situation was different on the track team. Nathan was far from the fastest guy there. He loved participating in the sport, though, and he knew he gave every race his best effort.

When he was waiting for his own events, Nathan watched his

teammates and their opponents intently and cheered his friends on. He was thrilled for his teammates whenever they won. He felt like the team was working together to achieve victory, and he loved being part of that joint effort. Still, he longed for personal victory on the track.

Nathan imagined what it must feel like to cross the finish line first. If only his legs were longer. Lets face it; Nathan was short, and that meant he was at a disadvantage. The schools his team competed against seemed to be filled with big, strong, long-legged runners.

Nathan's parents came to all the track meets to cheer him on. Sometimes he could hear them yelling, "Nice run, Nathan," as he passed the stands while often running in last place. He never felt embarrassed at his performance, exactly, but he knew everybody sitting in the stands realized that his parents were cheering for the kid who couldn't run as fast as the other guys. Somehow that made him feel bad for his parents. He wanted to win a race for them. He'd feel great if they could be cheering for the winning kid.

Still, he *was* on a winning team. Most of the time when the points were added up at the end of a meet, his school came out on top. That felt good, and it felt good to realize that his team-mates admired him. Every afternoon when school was over and practice began, in the locker room before the meet, during the event, and afterward, they made Nathan feel like an important part of the team; they made him feel like a winner.

Nathan's teammates understood his feelings about track bet-ter than anyone else. When it came to this sport, they had the most in common with him. They knew how hard he worked, how much he wanted to win, and how difficult it was to lose. They understood the physical challenge Nathan was up against, and each of them admired the fact that he never stopped trying.

After each meet at least one teammate would complement Nathan on his performance, and he always appreciated the comments from his coach.

"Don't worry, Nate," the coach would say. "That was a great run. Remember you're just a freshman and some of these guys are seniors. They've got a lot of experience under their belts. Your day is coming. Hang in there. If you keep training hard, you'll be a great runner someday." His coach was consistent in his encouragement and really seemed to appreciate having Nathan on the team.

WHEN Nathan and his friends were young children challenging each other to race, were they playing a game or participating in a sport? Perhaps it was a game then, but running became a sport when Nathan joined the high school track team.

What is the difference between a game and a sport? Both are fun, and both can be physical events requiring a set of skills. Some games and sports are played by teams, but others can be played by individuals. All sports are games, but all games are not sports.

Sometimes a sporting contest is a highly organized official event. Adults often form leagues to oversee sports, and they may be the ones in charge of a match between teams. A group of adults living in your neighborhood may decide to become affiliated with an even larger organization for this purpose. People who want to participate in the sport might have to apply and/or join the organization in order to do so. They may have to participate in tryouts where they must demonstrate their level of skill in the particular sport before being allowed to play. Often a particular company sponsors sports teams. An individual or a corporation may own professional teams. Members of sports teams usually wear uniforms. In the case of professional teams, they even get paid to participate in the sport. Sports also usually have spectators, while games seldom do.

Games are usually **spontaneous**, informal, and organized by the individuals playing them. Sports have rules that are written down and often strictly enforced. Sometimes officials are on the playing field watching every movement the players make to be certain none of the rules are broken. Games also have rules, but they are less formal. Sometimes children playing a game even change the rules to suit their mood and circumstances. Sports

Sports have spectators, while games that are not sports are seldom watched by a crowd.

Tennis is a sport with a long history.

teams have coaches who train the players. Games are usually learned by children from other children, and no formal training is needed to play.

Golf, tennis, and track are examples of sports that are played by individuals. A track team is composed of members who participate in various events on an individual basis. Running, jumping, pole-vaulting, **discus**, **shot put**, and javelin throwing are all events that take place during track meets.

But most well-known sports popular today are played by teams as a group, meaning that many members of the team participate in the sport at the same time on a playing field. Cooperation between team members is essential when engaging in this type of game. Basketball, football, field hockey, cricket, and soccer are all examples of team sports. These activities may have been games first, before they became sports.

BASKETBALL

Basketball is one of the most popular sports in America. This game was first played in Massachusetts, but it was invented by a Canadian named James Naismith. Members of the YMCA had been searching for an enjoyable athletic game that could be played indoor. In 1891, the first basketball game was played using a soccer ball. Players earned points for their team by putting the soccer ball through fruit baskets mounted on the wall. It was a humble beginning, but the enjoyment and popularity of basketball spread rapidly. By 1895 it was already being played in several colleges in the United States. By 1898 there was a professional basketball league. During the 1950s the sport was played around the world in 60 countries.

Not just players enjoy basketball. It is also enjoyed by millions of people who attend basketball games or watch them on television.

Basketball is not only a professional sport, however. It is also a folk tradition that is passed along in pick-up games across North America. In the game of H-O-R-S-E, for example, two players take turns shooting baskets; when one misses, he or she gains a letter from the word "horse." The first person to complete the word loses. In games like these, officials, official rules, paying audiences, and hierarchical control are all absent.

FOOTBALL

In the late 1800s, people began playing football in a manner similar to the way it is played today in the United States. In fact,

A CONTEMPORARY FOLK CELEBRATION

Holidays are an important part of folklore, a cycle of festivals that gives meaning and identity to people's lives. In our modern world, Super Bowl Sunday has become an annual event that includes many traditions. Each year people across North America hold informal parties where friends and family gather together to have a good time while they watch the game. They eat chicken wings, pizza, chips and dip, and other goodies convenient for picking up while watching the television.

the first professional football game was played in 1895. But football has origins that go back much farther than that. Football can trace its roots to rugby, which is still a popular sport on many college campuses as well as in many countries. In football's early days it was quite a dangerous activity, and players were injured or even died. In the early 1900s, several colleges were so concerned about injuries that they banned the sport. President Theodore Roosevelt was a fan of many active sports including football, and he decided that the game could be made safer. That's when a committee was organized that established several rules of play.

Although football was not particularly popular among the general public during the first few decades it was played professionally, today it is tremendously popular. Watching the annual Super Bowl has become a national and even international event.

RACKET GAMES

All racket sports seem to have come out of France in the Middle Ages. The original sport, "Jeu de Paume," was played with the hand; sometimes a net was used, sometimes a wall, and sometimes neither. Eventually, people started wearing gloves, then wrapping their hands, and ultimately they used a racket or paddle to hit the ball. This game eventually became tennis, a game that is played across North America. However, because you need a court to play this game, traditionally it has been a game of the elite. If you want to play tennis, you need to have enough money (or belong to a community with enough money) to have a place to play the game.

Other "less elite" racket games still exist today. For instance, badminton and Ping-Pong (or table tennis) are favorites of many young people.

The game played in America as squash came from a British game called rackets, which evolved from the court games of the late 18th and early 19th centuries; it was closely related to the handball-like game of "five." Rackets was played both inside with three or four walls and outside on a single wall. Like tennis, rackets was a game for the upper class. The courts themselves are the reason for this; they were expensive to construct and maintain and the game was expensive to play, since a seven-game match might use as many as

In the 19th century, lawn tennis was considered a suitable pastime for an upper-class afternoon.

100 balls. At current prices, that would mean each game would cost around $400.

Rackets was the main racket court game in Britain until the end of the 19th century, when players began to play with a punctured rackets ball—a squashed ball. In 1864, the school of Harrow constructed four courts, and squash rackets was officially created. The courts were much smaller and less expensive to construct, and the softer ball slowed play to the point where more people could participate in the sport. The game was less expensive to play; it could be learned more easily; and it had a social element to it that rackets lacked. While rackets was a sport for upper class males, many people began to enjoy squash rackets.

In the late 19th century, squash spread to Canada and the United States, mostly through boys' private schools. The game never caught on internationally, however. By the 1930s, squash rackets (more often called "squash") had spread only to the United States, Canada, and India. Today squash courts are uncommon in most regions of the United States, although New England and Northeastern communities are more apt to offer these facilities. In most areas, squash has become as "upper class" as the rackets it replaced.

Meanwhile, tennis, once the game of the rich, has become more and more popular. Most towns or schools offer at least outdoor tennis courts, and larger cities have indoor facilities

Ninepins was the colonial forerunner of bowling.

as well. Growing numbers of North Americans, both male and female, young and old, are finding that tennis is a fun way to exercise.

A NATIONAL PASTIME

Baseball is one sport that has become so familiar and well liked in the United States that it is known as the "national pastime." Baseball may very well be the favorite professional sport in America. But it's unofficial title was also bestowed upon it because most citizens of the United States have participated in the sport, not just as spectators, but as players—many from the time they were small children.

Across North America, families enroll their children in T-ball, the most elementary form of baseball, at a very young age. A lightweight bat is used, and the ball is placed on a T so that every child can easily hit it and have an opportunity to run the bases. After "graduating" from T-ball, children often join Little League. The United States is not the only country that participates in

SAFE HIT

BRAND

Texas
VEGETABLES

PACKED & SHIPPED BY
GULF DISTRIBUTING CO.
WESLACO · TEXAS · U.S.A.

Baseball has been so popular across North America that it even permeated advertising.

Little League. First organized in 1939, Little League is well established in many countries including Canada. Each year, teams across the world participate in play-off and championship games to determine the top teams.

There are countless other baseball leagues that people participate in throughout elementary school, high school, college, and beyond. Sometimes companies sponsor teams composed of workers. Adults living in the same community often establish teams.

The highest level of the sport is composed of professional players in the major leagues, but there are also minor leagues in baseball. These minor league teams are sometimes referred to as the "farm teams" of major league teams. They offer a place where players who are not yet skillful enough to play in the major leagues can improve their skills, with the hope of someday moving up to the major leagues.

Some cities that are too small to support a major league team have a minor league team that offers much excitement for families living in the area. A night at the local ballpark can be a real social event. Between innings there may be base races, where children attending the game will run against the team mascot; sometimes there are fireworks after the game; or there might be a carousel to ride on before the game begins. Then of course there is the game itself. Com-

The origins of baseball are not completely certain, but many historians believe it is derived from cricket (which is still popular in England and South Africa among other countries) and a game called rounders. Both games were brought to the United States when it was still a colony. In fact, variations of baseball were played in America as early as the late 1700s. Baseball gets its name from the bases that have been used to play the game since some time between 1840 and 1845.

The World Series, which determines the championship team, has a long history as well. The first series of games to determine the champion team of the major leagues was conducted in 1884, and the first modern version of the World Series was held in 1903.

posed of nine or more innings, the game can take some time, but it passes quickly for spectators due to the excitement of the game, play-by-play announcing, music coming from the loudspeakers, and refreshments like hot dogs and peanuts, all of which have come to be associated with a night at the baseball game.

A baseball game is full of traditions, such as the singing of the National Anthem before the game begins. Then there's the Seventh-Inning Stretch, when spectators rise to their feet and sing another sort of anthem—"Take Me Out to the Ball Game." Spectators also have various cheers that have become traditional, including the "Wave," when spectators leap to their feet and throw up their hands in a progressive surge of human arms that makes its way around the stadium. Spectators may also

BASEBALL'S "ANTHEM"

Take me out to the ball game,
Take me out to the field.
Buy me some peanuts and Crackerjacks,
I don't care if we never come back.
So it's root, root, root, for the home team.
If they don't win it's shame.
And it's one, two, three strikes, you're out!
At the old ball game.

CANADA'S NATIONAL SPORT

The United States is not the only country to place great pride and importance upon a sport. In 1867, Canada declared lacrosse to be its national sport, and it remains so today. Lacrosse is truly an American game for it has its origins on this continent, having been invented by Native Americans.

Native Americans often engaged in athletic contests. In the eastern part of America (and in some areas along the Pacific coast), a ball game was popular. The game was called *baggataway*, and it was played with sticks that had a loop on one end with a net fastened to it. The net was used to catch the ball. It was French Canadians who first used the term *la crosse* to refer to this playing stick.

Lacrosse is not just played in Canada. Though not as well known as some other sports, it has been played in the United States since the late 1800s. Today it is played on many college campuses.

In Canada the game changed somewhat in the 1930s when it was adapted for indoor as well as outdoor play.

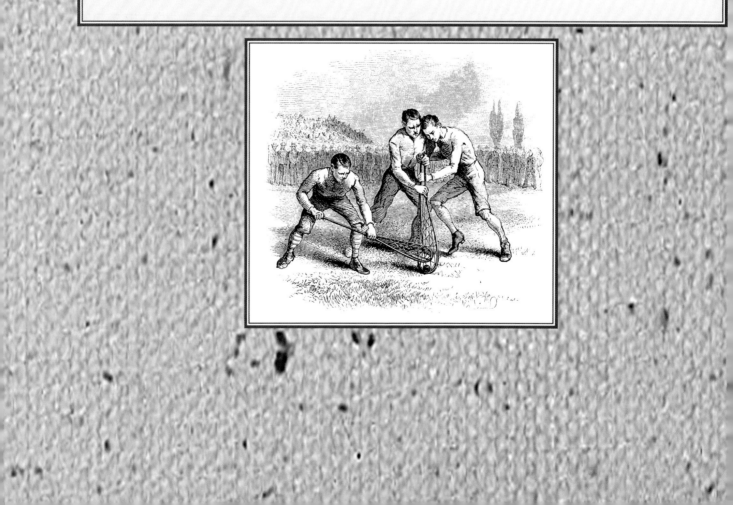

 bounce balloons around the stadium, increasing their sense of togetherness and camaraderie. Then there are traditions observed by the players, such as tossing the ball around the "horn," when outfielders throw the ball from player to player. Players also have many superstitions: if a player performs well one night with his cap on backward, he may play that way for the rest of the season—or a team member may play with one sock half down as a good luck charm. All of these customs combine together to make a baseball game a richly satisfying experience, replete with familiar traditions.

New York City has played a particularly important role in the history of baseball. For one thing, it was the home of both the Knickerbockers and the New York Nine. These two ball clubs played what some people think was the first modern baseball game in Hoboken, New Jersey, in 1846, although professional baseball was not introduced until 1869. The Knickerbockers were also the first baseball team to wear uniforms.

Baseball reflects much of what is best in North American culture. Its atmosphere of fair play, cooperation, and togetherness make it truly deserving of its title: a national pastime.

CLEARLY, sports are an important part of our game traditions. In our fitness-conscious world, sports play an increasing important role. However, as Nathan found at the beginning of this chapter, a person's age and size can be an advantage or disadvantage in some of the sports people play. Nathan was at a disadvantage for track because he was young and short.

But sometimes being older or larger can work against an indi-

vidual. A 40-year-old man might have a hard time playing basketball with a group of 19-year-olds, for example. A person
weighing 200 pounds might have difficulty participating in a
race with individuals weighing less than 150 pounds.

Generally speaking, experience and skill are developed and
grow as we play games. Usually, the more sports a person plays,
the better athlete he or she becomes. For example, a person who
plays chess twice a week will probably get progressively better at
chess. She or he may also be getting better at other games. That's
because the patience and strategy being learned while playing
chess might transfer over to other games. People who play base-

Fencing was once a popular sport, even for women, but today its popularity has faded.

NATIVE AMERICAN SPORTS

A game called chunky was popular among some Eastern tribes. Equipment needed to play the game consisted of a pole with a curve in one end and a stone disk.

Races, both on foot and on horseback, were some of the ways that Native Americans living on the plains had fun.

Some Native American women participated in a simple form of football.

Today's American Indians continue to enjoy their cultural sports heritage.

ball once a week may find their tennis game has improved even though they play it less frequently. They have been developing better hand-and-eye coordination when swinging at the baseball, and that could be of benefit in other games.

Each time we play, we gain knowledge and experience. That knowledge and experience is available to us when we play subsequent sports. Still, while most people enjoy playing games, not too many people actually enjoy losing them. When we play a game, it's only natural that we prefer to win. But no one can win every game they play. We have the best experience when we learn to enjoy the sport for the fun and *camaraderie* it offers, regardless of whether we win or lose. Learning to lose a game with grace and dignity is part of learning how to interact well with others.

Today, some *sociologists* wonder if many children and young adults are enrolled in so many organized sports that they have lost the time to play games. Since sports are more organized and less creative, these researchers fear that kids may be missing an opportunity to develop their imaginations, as well as interpersonal skills. Sports do, however, provide an opportunity for children to learn cooperation, commitment, and persistence.

What do you think? Does your life hold the right balance between sports and games?

Adults and young people both need to play.

SEVEN

Children's Games
Today
Fun and Play

Children's play is more spontaneous, less structured than games.

CHILDREN PLAY. They play games—and they simply play, with no structure or rules to restrict them. A stick, a penny, a piece of paper, or nothing at all can fill a child's hours with amusement. And while children may be the experts on play, most adults still remember how to play as well.

Play belongs to the part of our lives where we are simply ourselves, without rules, without masks, without any "shoulds" or "ought-tos." Play is free; it often engages our imagination and fantasies; and most of all play is fun.

Play is also one of the ways children learn about their world. As a child grows, she connects herself to the world through play. Play helps her express herself—and play helps her internalize all she is learning about her environment. Eventually, it will teach her how to interact with others. As the child's play expands into formal games, she will learn sequencing skills, socialization skills, and countless other valuable tactics for understanding the world. Traditional games will teach her about teamwork, about group values, and about unspoken lifestyle rules.

These traditional games share some things in common:

- They are played by children just for the pleasure of playing; children themselves decide when, where, and how these games are played.
- They have rules that are easy to understand, remember, and obey—and which can be negotiated as needed.
- They require little if any expensive materials.
- They are easy to share.
- They can be played any time, anywhere.

Many of these games involve chants or rhythms. These encourage children's language development. They teach them ways of telling stories and communicating. These rhythmic verbal expressions are often accompanied by body movements as well, helping children grow and develop both intellectually and physically.

> For the player everything is possible: every single thing may be a number of things. For a child, anything he wants comes true. Play is the kingdom of the imagination, where nothing is impossible. Everything is possible.
>
> —*Supúlveda Llanos*

HANDCLAPPING CHANTS

A Sailor Went to Sea

A sailor went to sea, sea, sea.
To see what he could see, see, see.
But all that he could see, see, see
Was the bottom of the deep blue sea, sea, sea.

Atchi Katchi Liberatchi

Atchi Katchi Liberatchi,
I love you.
Take a peach, take a pear, take the teacher's underwear.
No more books, no more looks, no more teacher's dirty looks.
Olé!

Children's swings existed on the Island of Crete in 1600 BC, and hopscotch was played in ancient Greece as well. Blindman's buff and marbles date back at least 2,000 years.

THE SHORT-LEGGED SAILOR

*Have you ever, ever, ever in your short-legged life
seen a short-legged sailor with a short-legged wife?*

*No, I've never, never, never in my short-legged life
seen a short-legged sailor with a short-legged wife.*

*Have you ever, ever, ever in your long legged life
seen a long legged sailor with a long legged wife?*

*Play provides children with
physical exercise.*

No, I've never, never, never, in my long-legged life
seen a long-legged sailor with a long legged wife.

Have you ever, ever, ever, in your knock-kneed life
seen a knock-kneed sailor with a knock-kneed wife?

No, I've never, never, never in my knock-kneed life
seen a knock-kneed sailor with a knock-kneed wife.

Have you ever, ever, ever in your short-legged life
seen a long-legged sailor with a knock-kneed wife?

No, I've never, never, never in my short-legged life
seen a long-legged sailor with a knock-kneed wife.

JUMP-ROPE RHYMES

Down by the River
Down by the river, down by the sea,
Johnny broke a bottle and blamed it on me.
I told Ma, Ma told Pa,
Johnny got a spanking so ha ha ha.
How many spankings did Johnny get?
1, 2, 3, . . .

Spanish Dancer
Not last night but the night before,
Twenty-four robbers came knocking at my door
I asked them what they wanted, and this is what they said:
Spanish dancer, do the splits, the twist,

the turnaround and touch the ground, and out the back door.
Spanish dancer, please come back, back, sit on a tack, read a
  book and do not look,
1, 2, 3, . . .

Three Blind Mice

A horse, a flea, and three blind mice,
sat on a curbstone shooting dice.
The horse, he slipped and fell on the flea.
The flea said "Whoops, there's a horse on me."

As adults, few people play jump-rope or handclapping games. But games should not only be for the young but the young at heart as well. Games are metaphors for dealing with real life. They give us physical exercise; they challenge our minds; and they fill our lives with fun.

DOGGY, WHERE'S YOUR BONE?

This indoor game is good for a rainy day. One child sits in a chair with his back to the others in the group. A pencil or some other object (the "bone") is placed under his chair. Then someone in the group sneaks up and steals the bone, and hides it in her pocket or somewhere on her person. The group sings,

Doggy, Doggy, where's your bone?
Somebody's stole it from your home.
Guess who it might be.

Then the "dog" has 3 chances to guess who took the bone. If he guesses right, he gets to be Doggy again, but if he guesses wrong the person with the bone takes his place.

Pool is a game that can help us better understand the principles of physics.

EIGHT

Reflections of the Real World

Games That Offer Us a Deeper Vision

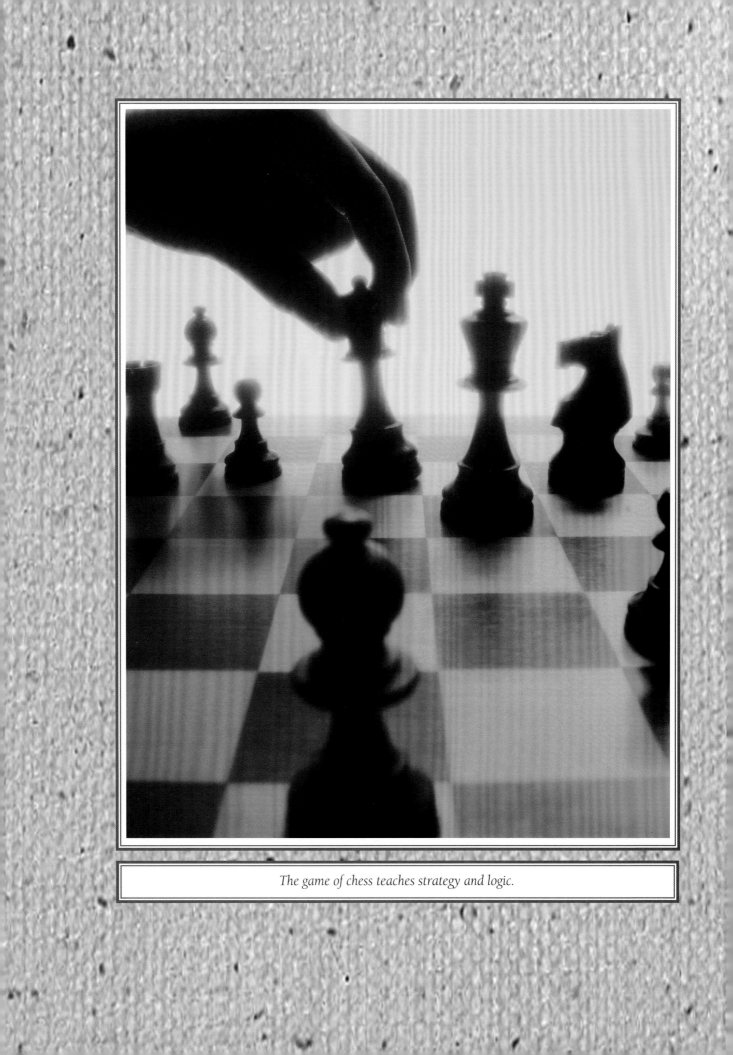

The game of chess teaches strategy and logic.

SATURDAY, JUNE 11, was destined to be a day filled with fantastic events in the Becker household. The twins would be turning seven that day. Evie and Benjamin were anxious for their day to arrive. They knew there would be a party. What they didn't know was that their parents wanted the day to be truly memorable. Their mom had decided on "a rip-roaring old-fashioned birthday" as the theme for the party, and had been busy for weeks making arrangements for special surprises.

A neighbor would be dressed in a clown suit teaching magic tricks. A nearby farmer planned to hitch his tractor to the old hay wagon and give the kids a ride. While digging through stuff stored in the basement, Laura, the twins' mother, had found an old Pin the Tail on the Donkey game, and she was resurrecting it for the party.

"Don't you think they're a little old for that?" asked her husband.

"I guess they are, but I think some of the kids might enjoy a round or two. It's always fun to watch the blindfolded person try to get the tail in the right place. Heck, some of the parents might even want to try it," Laura replied.

On Wednesday, the twins' grandmother arrived to collect the children for the remainder of the week so their parents could get ready for the party. The children had their bags packed before Grandma Bernice arrived, but Ben had to run back into the house for one forgotten thing.

"Sorry," he apologized as he dashed back to the car. "I forgot a paper and pencil. I thought Evie might like to play hangman in the car." Ben was a master at all games played with a paper and pencil.

"Since we're in the car, why don't we look out the car window and try to spot something?" Evie asked. She preferred to look out the car window and see who could see the most license plates from different states.

"Let's play paper, rock, scissors to decide who picks the game," Ben suggested, and Evie agreed.

> Paper, rock, scissors is played in many countries. It is called Jan Ken Po in Japan, where it has been played for centuries.

Wednesday evening, the twins' parents made a trip of their own to the local department store to pick out party favors. "Let's each pick out something we liked to play with when we were kids," suggested Laura as they searched store shelves. "Oh gosh, here it is. I've found it already—jacks! I loved playing jacks when I was a kid. I don't care for the rubber ball though. Golf balls have a much better bounce. I'm going to buy a package of recycled golf balls to go with these. It's your turn, Paul. What did you like to play with when you were growing up?"

"Hmmm, let's see, I know, I'm getting yo-yos. I'll teach everyone how to 'walk the dog.' I was great at yo-yo tricks when I was young."

> Games are the most elevated form of investigation.
> —*Albert Einstein*

"Hey, you know what? I'm going to make a piñata for the party," Laura announced.

After purchasing all of the party "necessities," the twins' parents left the department store and headed for home. "What games do you think we should play? We could have a baseball game, but the kids play baseball every week. I'd rather play some more unusual games. What do you think?" asked Laura.

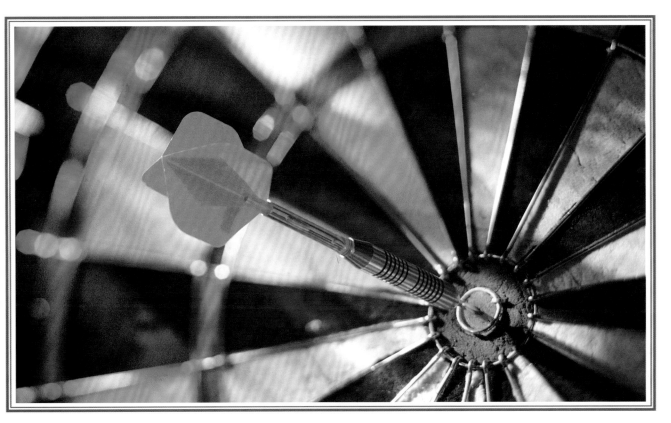

Playing darts is like shooting a little arrow without the bow. It developed in the 16th century, and today it is a game often played in bars.

"How about kick-the-can? I always enjoyed that when I was a kid," Paul responded.

When Grandma Bernice pulled her car into the driveway Saturday afternoon, everything seemed quiet, but when Ben and Evie opened the door to their house, the yell of "surprise" was deafening. Kids and parents began emerging from every conceivable hiding place. Streamers crisscrossed over their heads, and helium-filled balloons hung in the air. People talked and laughed as they began to play the various games organized by the twins' parents. As Laura listened to the happy roar of people having a good time, she knew the party was definitely a success.

BIRTHDAYS have always been great occasions for game playing, but people have never needed a special occasion to play a game. All they need is time to be together and relaxed, and some type of game playing will probably begin. But the variety of games available, from which they will decide what to play, is seemingly endless.

Many games are competitive; others are not. Some games provide a **forum** where children and/or adults can work out aggressions; others do not. Games are as diverse as people's imaginations, and they can be as creative as the people who are playing them. Games can be entirely physical, or entirely intellectual, or a combination of the two. They can be purely based on chance, or they can be based on skill.

According to Phil Wiswell, the author of *Kids' Games* (1987, Doubleday), the worldwide popularity of kick-the-can "may be traced to the industrial revolution and the invention of canning processes," since the only piece of equipment necessary to play the game is a tin can.

In the 1800s, croquet was a popular lawn game for summer afternoons. People enjoyed it so much that they made a parlor version of the same game to be played indoors.

Computer games created by individuals can be played with strangers from across the world over the Internet. Will these become our newest folk games?

Realizing the importance games play in the social development of individuals, might violent video games provide negative social development? What do you think?

Sometimes games reflect the culture of the people playing them, but many games are cross-cultural. Some games can even function as a universal language because people can communicate and interact with each other through the game even when those playing don't speak the same language.

Games are important to the social development of human beings. Today, the importance of game playing is being realized as evidenced by the use of game therapy for individuals who have experienced certain types of trauma in their lives. The rehabilitation of child soldiers in some countries is just one example of how game therapy is being used.

Scholars in many disciplines, including mathematics, history, psychology, and anthropology, have studied games and their effects. For instance, games of strategy, like checkers and chess, provide researchers with models for studying the decision-making process as it relates to many situations—including business, war, and even marriage. Games of chance like dice and roulette have contributed to "probability theory," the statistical analysis of outcomes for a variety of social problems.

Games help individuals develop physically, mentally, and socially. They provide a safe place to learn about social relationships and to develop our own character. Though they may seem at times to be simple and even unimportant, games play an extremely important role in the growth of healthy human beings.

Games unite any playground.

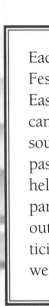

Each summer the Kutztown Folk Festival is held for one week in Eastern Pennsylvania. There, visitors can immerse themselves in sights, sounds, foods, and activities of the past. Find out if a similar venue is held near your hometown. Tell your parents about it, and consider a family outing there. You may be able to participate in some games just as they were played in a past era.

In short, games are recreational; games are good exercise for mind and body; and most of all, games are fun. But even more than that, games are the means to serious achievements for our culture. They are rooted in hundreds of years of folk tradition—and they continue to teach their lessons today.

Further Reading

Brandreth, Gyles. *The World's Best Indoor Games*. New York: Pantheon Books, 1981.

Falkner, David. *Great Time Coming: The Life of Jackie Robinson from Baseball to Birmingham*. New York: Simon & Schuster, 1995.

Jones, Bessie and Bess Lomax Hawes. *Step It Down: Games, Plays, Songs, and Stories from the Afro-American Heritage*. Athens: University of Georgia, 1987.

Millen, Nina. *Children's Games from Many Lands*. New York: Friendship Press, 1995.

Rader, Benjamin. *American Sports: From the Age of Folk Games to the Age of Televised Sports*. New York: Prentice Hall, 1997.

Sierra, Judy and Kaminski, Robert. *Children's Traditional Games*, Phoenix, Ariz.: Oryx, 1995.

Wiswell, Phil. *Kids' Games*. Garden City, N.Y.: Doubleday, 1987.

For More Information

Folk Games
www.iearn.org/projects/folkgames.html

Children's Games
www.gameskidsplay.net

Games
digilander.iol.it/cfgames2000/land_laura.html
www.education-world.com/atech/tech050.html
www.deepfun.com/resources.htm

Racket Games
www.geograph.ccsu.edu/harmony/atlas/squash.htm

Glossary

Camaraderie   A spirit of friendly good fellowship.

Classic   Traditional, enduring, never out of style.

Discus   A track-and-field sport where a round disc is hurled.

Forum   A medium or opportunity.

Immigrants   People who leave their homeland to live in another country.

Jousting   Fighting on horseback with lances.

Repertory   Supply of skills.

Revered   Honored.

Shot put   A track-and-field sport where a metal sphere is heaved for distance.

Socialization   The process of making a person fit for a social environment.

Sociologists   People who study society and social relationships.

Spontaneous   Occurring on impulse without any external pressure.

Suits   All the playing cards in a pack with the same symbols.

Index

Biographies

Joyce Libal is a graduate of the University of Wisconsin, Green Bay. She lives and works as a magazine editor in northeastern Pennsylvania.

Dr. Alan Jabbour is a folklorist who served as the founding director of the American Folklife Center at the Library of Congress from 1976 to 1999. Previously, he began the grant-giving program in folk arts at the National Endowment for the Arts (1974–76). A native of Jacksonville, Florida, he was trained at the University of Miami (B.A.) and Duke University (M.A., Ph.D.). A violinist from childhood on, he documented oldtime fiddling in the Upper South in the 1960s and 1970s. A specialist in instrumental folk music, he is known as a fiddler himself, an art he acquired directly from elderly fiddlers in North Carolina, Virginia, and West Virginia. He has taught folklore and folk music at UCLA and the University of Maryland and has published widely in the field.